GET INFORMED—STAY INFORMED

LEGALIZING MARIJUANA

Natalie Hyde

CRABTREE
PUBLISHING COMPANY
WWW.CRABTREEBOOKS.COM

Author: Natalie Hyde
Series research and development: Reagan Miller
Editor-in-chief: Lionel Bender
Editors: Simon Adams, Ellen Rodger
Proofreaders: Laura Booth, Crystal Sikkens
Project coordinator: Melissa Boyce
Design and photo research: Ben White
Production: Kim Richardson
Production coordinator and Prepress technician: Margaret Amy Salter
Print coordinator: Katherine Berti
Consultant: Emily Drew, Public Librarian, B.F.A., M.S.-LIS

Produced for Crabtree Publishing Company by Bender Richardson White

Photographs and reproductions: Alamy: 4–5 (age footstock), 18 (Military Collection), 29 (wendy connett), 36–37 (Paul Brown); Getty Images: 8–9 (Jeff Rotman), 11 (Don MacKinnon), 20–21 (Joe Amon), 38–39, 40–41 (Hero Images); Shutterstock: 1, 30–31 (Lifestyle discover), 10, 37 (arindambanerjee), 12–13 (Doug Mclean), 16–17 Tunatura), 22–23 (Shawn Goldberg), 25 (Flapas), 26–27 (Solarisys), 32–33 (rblfmr), 34 (Adam Melnyk), 35 (Photographee.eu), 42–43 (Monkey Business Images); Topfoto: 14, 19 (The Image Works), 15 (Harold Chapman); Icons & heading band: shutterstock.com

Diagrams: Stefan Chabluk, using the following as sources of data: p. 7t Colorado Department of Revenue. p. 7b RoyalQueenSeeds.com. p. 17 U.S. National Conference of State Legislatures. p. 20 American Civil Liberties Union/Bureau of Justice. p. 24 Insurance Institute of Highway Safety/Politifact.com. p. 27 Gallup/ Statista.com. p. 29 Leafly/Statista.com. p. 33 Gallup poll/Canadian Government p. 34 Pew Research Center and Gallup.com. p. 41 Drugwarfacts.org/Drugpolicy.ca.

Library and Archives Canada Cataloguing in Publication

Title: Legalizing marijuana / Natalie Hyde.
Names: Hyde, Natalie, 1963- author.
Series: Get informed--stay informed.
Description: Series statement: Get informed, stay informed | Includes bibliographical references and index.
Identifiers: Canadiana (print) 2019023671X | Canadiana (ebook) 20190236728 | ISBN 9780778772736 (hardcover) | ISBN 9780778772781 (softcover) | ISBN 9781427124661 (HTML)
Subjects: LCSH: Drug legalization—United States—Juvenile literature. | LCSH: Marijuana—Social aspects—United States—Juvenile literature. | LCSH: Marijuana—Law and legislation—United States—Juvenile literature. | LCSH: Drug legalization—Canada—Juvenile literature. | LCSH: Marijuana—Social aspects—Canada—Juvenile literature. | LCSH: Marijuana—Law and legislation—Canada—Juvenile literature.
Classification: LCC HV5822.M3 .H93 2020 | DDC j344.7304/233—dc23

Library of Congress Cataloging-in-Publication Data

Names: Hyde, Natalie, 1963- author.
Title: Legalizing marijuana / Natalie Hyde.
Description: New York, NY : Crabtree Publishing Company, [2020] | Series: Get informed, stay informed | Includes bibliographical references and index.
Identifiers: LCCN 2019053221 (print) | LCCN 2019053222 (ebook) | ISBN 9780778772736 (hardcover) | ISBN 9780778772781 (paperback) | ISBN 9781427124661 (ebook)
Subjects: LCSH: Marijuana--Social aspects--United States--Juvenile literature. | Marijuana--Law and legislation--United States--Juvenile literature.
Classification: LCC HV5822.M3 .H93 2020 (print) | LCC HV5822.M3 (ebook) | DDC 344.7304/233--dc23
LC record available at https://lccn.loc.gov/2019053221
LC ebook record available at https://lccn.loc.gov/2019053222

Crabtree Publishing Company
www.crabtreebooks.com 1-800-387-7650

Printed in the U.S.A./032020/CG20200127

Published in Canada
Crabtree Publishing
616 Welland Ave.
St. Catharines, ON
L2M 5V6

Published in the United States
Crabtree Publishing
PMB 59051
350 Fifth Avenue, 59th Floor
New York, NY 10118

Published in the United Kingdom
Crabtree Publishing
Maritime House
Basin Road North, Hove
BN41 1WR

Published in Australia
Crabtree Publishing
Unit 3 – 5 Currumbin Court
Capalaba
QLD 4157

CONTENTS

1 THE MARIJUANA ISSUE

Marijuana is a product of the cannabis plant. It has been illegal to use in North America for almost 100 years. Before that, it was sold as a herbal medicine. Many countries and states are now legalizing cannabis, but this has led to confusion among some people who don't understand why a drug the government formerly thought was dangerous enough to prohibit (much like cocaine) is now considered safe for use.

▶ Norwegian tourists visit a marijuana store in Denver, Colorado, to buy cannabis products. About half of all **recreational** marijuana sold in Colorado is to tourists.

QUESTIONS TO ASK

Within this book are three types of boxes with questions to help your critical thinking about legalizing marijuana. The icons will help you identify them.

THE CENTRAL ISSUES
Learning about the main points of information.

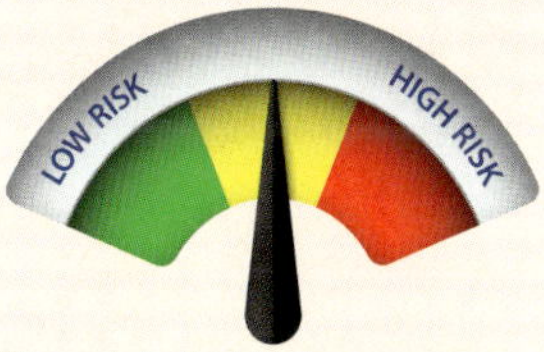

WHAT'S AT STAKE?
Helping you determine how the issue will affect you.

ASK YOUR OWN QUESTIONS
Prompts for gaps in your understanding.

Marijuana is often referred to as cannabis. This name is also used for a related product, hemp. The hemp form of the cannabis plant is valued not only for its herbal medicine, but also for its use in making rope, cloth, paper, paint, biofuel, and animal feed. Regarding the **legalization** of marijuana, both forms of cannabis are involved.

MEDICINAL USES—AND ABUSES

A drug is any substance that changes how your body works. Alcohol is a drug. So is tobacco. Both are regulated by laws. A medicine is a drug used to treat a disease or disorder of the body. Marijuana is a drug, and in some areas of the world, it is also used as a medicine. Information about if and how drugs and medicines should be used, and how they react with the mind and body, is constantly being updated. **Addiction** and deaths due to their misuse are rising. Many people fear that using marijuana will add to this by leading to other drug use.

Other people are relieved that marijuana is beginning to be legalized and accepted. They see marijuana as an **effective** medication to help with symptoms that are not helped by other medicines. Scientists and doctors are always looking for better pain medication with fewer and/or safer side effects. Determining if cannabis products are a new method of treating problems or lead to addiction and the threat of overdose, is the heart of the debate of legalizing marijuana.

> “*I want to say this just as clearly and as forthrightly as I can—marijuana prohibition, criminal prohibition of marijuana, is a complete failure.*”
> Former U.S. district attorney John McKay, April 18, 2012

Knowing about cannabis, its uses, and dangers, is vital for us to make choices in our lives. What we know—or don't know—affects what we consider safe to use. New studies and research on the effects of cannabis and the chemicals made from it are adding to our understanding all the time. Having the latest and most accurate information is key. For example, knowing how cannabis affects brain function and reaction times has led to new regulations for people operating machinery at work or driving a car. In areas where marijuana use is legal, new laws have been written including THC levels linked to driving "under the influence."

Learning about legalizing marijuana can be **intimidating**. There is a lot of information, and some of it goes against what we may have heard or learned before. There is also a **stigma** in **society** concerning talking about drugs and drug use. This may make it hard to approach parents, teachers, or law enforcement to ask questions and get answers.

THE INFLUENCE OF CONTEXT

Our views about legalizing marijuana, like any topic, can change over time. Behavior that was once considered unthinkable or unacceptable, such as smoking a **joint**, may now seem harmless or even beneficial. The time, place, and circumstances in which that information is created is called its **context**. Context helps explain how the same data can be interpreted differently in other countries or as society changes. A study on the effects of marijuana written at about the time of **Prohibition** almost 100 years ago will be very different from the same study during the 1960s when marijuana use became more common. By being aware of the context in which information is created, you can allow for any slant or focus when reading it.

DRUG DATABASE

Cannabis is a type of tall, flowering plant. It is also the name used for specific cannabis products—hemp and marijuana.

Marijuana is a type of cannabis that contains chemicals that give people an uplifting feeling called a "**high**."

Hemp is a form of the cannabis plant with medicinal and commercial uses.

THC is short for *delta-9-tetrahydrocannabinol,* the chemical in cannabis plants that makes people high.

Cannabinoids are chemicals in cannabis plants that are used to treat body symptoms.

Gateway drugs are those that some doctors believe can lead to using stronger, more dangerous, drugs.

Decriminalization is when something is no longer treated as a crime.

Legalization is making something illegal, now legal.

Overdose happens when a person takes too much of a drug, leading to health problems and even death.

Heroin is an illegal and highly addictive drug made from the seeds of the poppy plant.

Ecstasy is an illegal, powerful, artificial, mind-altering drug.

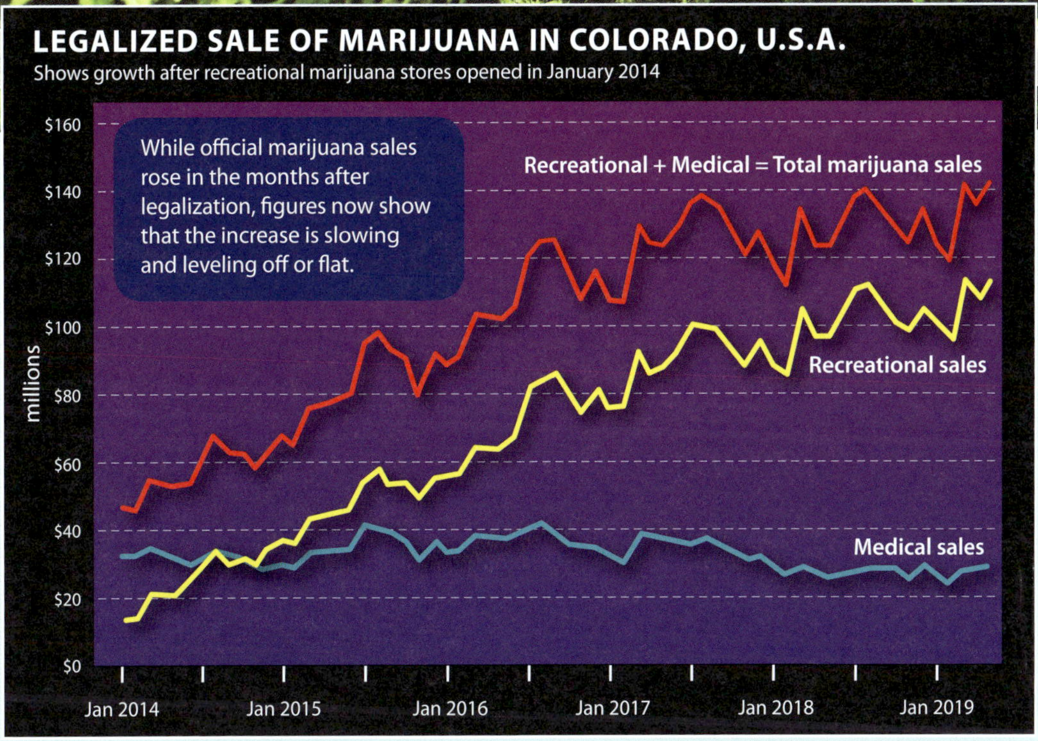
LEGALIZED SALE OF MARIJUANA IN COLORADO, U.S.A.
Shows growth after recreational marijuana stores opened in January 2014
While official marijuana sales rose in the months after legalization, figures now show that the increase is slowing and leveling off or flat.
Recreational + Medical = Total marijuana sales
Recreational sales
Medical sales
millions
$160
$140
$120
$100
$80
$60
$40
$20
$0
Jan 2014
Jan 2015
Jan 2016
Jan 2017
Jan 2018
Jan 2019

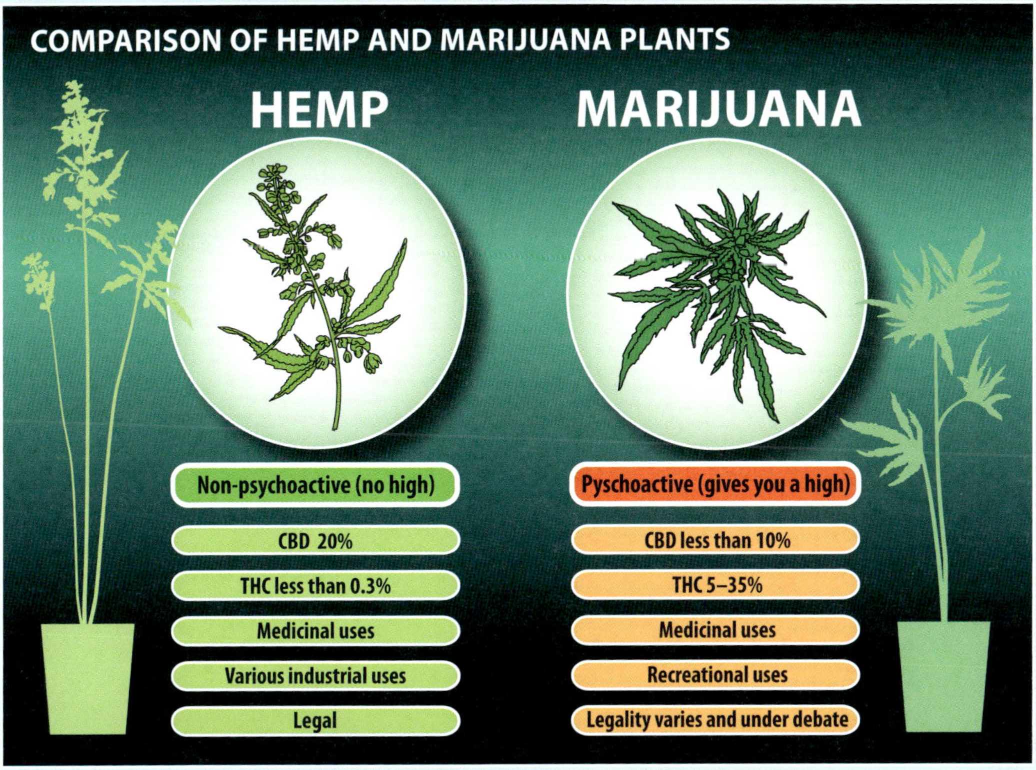
COMPARISON OF HEMP AND MARIJUANA PLANTS
HEMP
MARIJUANA
Non-psychoactive (no high)
CBD 20%
THC less than 0.3%
Medicinal uses
Various industrial uses
Legal
Pyschoactive (gives you a high)
CBD less than 10%
THC 5–35%
Medicinal uses
Recreational uses
Legality varies and under debate

2 HOW TO GET INFORMED

The starting point for understanding any topic is to become familiar with key players, background information, and vocabulary. The debate surrounding legalizing marijuana has a long history. There is a lot of information going back many **decades**. Gathering a wide variety of material will allow you to have a good overview of the subject.

▶ The flower buds are the part of the cannabis plant people smoke as marijuana. Different plant varieties have different levels of THC in their flowers.

KEY PLAYERS

NORML stands for the National Organization for the Reform of Marijuana Laws. It is a cannabis-rights organization based in the United States. It has branches in other countries, including Canada, New Zealand, Ireland, France, and the United Kingdom. It was founded in 1970 by Keith Stroup.

NORML holds seminars and conferences about marijuana and works toward its mission to legalize responsible use by adults. Its website provides a list of lawyers to help people charged with possession or use. It also produces a newsletter and runs a blog to provide information to the public.

DEALING WITH BIAS

Information can be slanted not only by the context, but also by the person or people creating it. New marijuana growers want to keep profits high and costs down. Governments have a duty to protect **citizens**, but also see legal marijuana as a way to increase tax revenue. Law enforcement is interested in keeping down drug crime and it needs to balance the rights of citizens with upholding laws. Patients want legal medicines that are effective and inexpensive to reduce pain and keep them healthy.

Each of these groups views and reports on the issue from its own perspective or focus—creating **bias**. Bias is not always bad, but it does color the conclusions of each group. Sorting out who and what to believe can be confusing. Recognizing bias while **analyzing** data will help you stay **objective**.

TIME AND PLACE RULE

It might take a lot of careful research to find a range of perspectives on the topic, and the most current studies. Sometimes articles and reports base their details and conclusions on outdated or unchecked facts. Many researchers use the **Time and Place Rule** to help them **evaluate** and select **source material**. The rule states that the closer in time to an event the material is created, the more likely it is to be accurate and reliable.

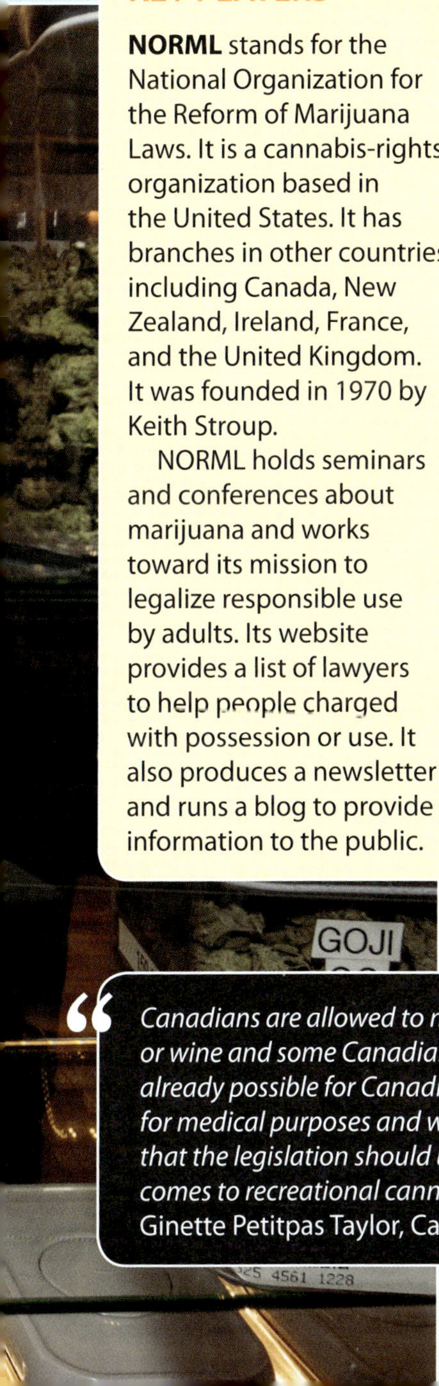

> *Canadians are allowed to make beer at home or wine and some Canadians grow tobacco. It's already possible for Canadians to grow cannabis for medical purposes and we absolutely believe that the legislation should be consistent when it comes to recreational cannabis.*
> Ginette Petitpas Taylor, Canadian politician, 2018

SOURCE MATERIALS

Getting informed with accurate information about a subject as possibly life-threatening as our use of drugs and medicines, is not always easy or straightforward. Information is not always collected in one place. Nor is it always in the same form. Information can be written, oral, auditory—sound recordings—or visual, as art, photographs, social media, movies, even graffiti.

Information about marijuana can be found online in web publications, newscasts, and podcasts. Libraries have books, magazines, journals, and textbooks on the topic. Newspapers online and in print—such as *The Globe and Mail, The New York Times,* and *The Washington Post*—report on new drug-related developments or problems. Government and health services' websites often have **statistics** and graphs. Doctors' offices and pharmacies have pamphlets and booklets that can answer health questions.

WHAT'S AT STAKE?

Sometimes "recommended reading lists" are created for students or adults to learn about a topic. Is this an unbiased source of information? If not, why?

▼ The Lift & Co. Expo in Toronto, Canada, offers an opportunity for the public to ask questions of health professionals and cannabis producers about marijuana. It is held each year to promote cannabis use.

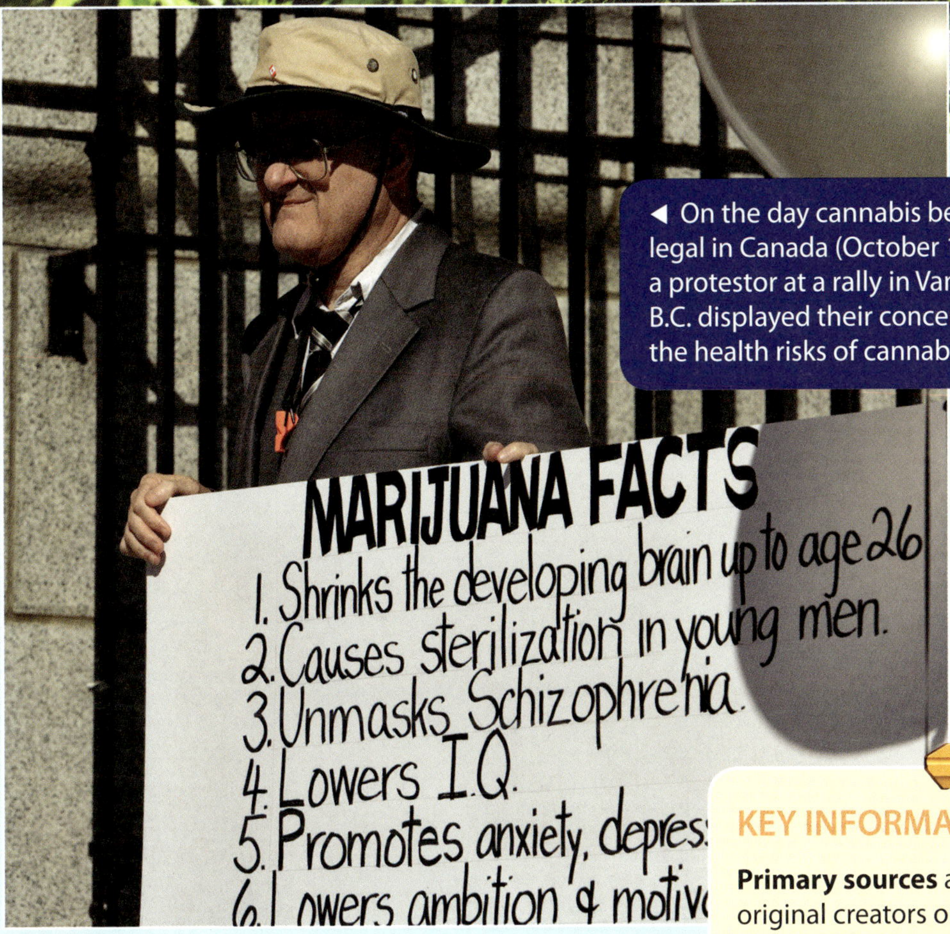

◀ On the day cannabis became legal in Canada (October 17, 2018), a protestor at a rally in Vancouver, B.C. displayed their concerns about the health risks of cannabis use.

A STRATEGY FOR UNDERSTANDING

It is always helpful to familiarize yourself with how we arrived at the point we are at today by following a timeline of events. (See marijuana timeline on page 15.) People's attitudes or understanding of an issue can change direction after a new discovery, a tragedy, or a threat. You should also learn the words and terms that relate to the issue so you can join in the conversation.

When discussing legalizing marijuana, it is important to understand different types of drugs, legal terms, signs and symptoms of addiction, and even slang used when talking about it. You should also consider the views of the key players in the debate and consider all sides of the issue, even if you don't agree with all of them.

KEY INFORMATION

Primary sources are the original creators or owners of information, for example, a scientific study of the types and levels of cannabinoids in different varieties of marijuana.
Secondary sources are reports, analyses, and interpretations of the primary sources such as studies comparing those levels to patients' levels of pain relief.
Tertiary sources are summaries or databases of primary and secondary information. They include Wikipedia articles or entries in encyclopedias.

3 LEGALIZING MARIJUANA

Marijuana is also known as pot, weed, grass, ganja, Mary Jane, and many other slang terms. It is a greenish-gray mixture of flowers of the *Cannabis sativa* plant. People smoke marijuana in hand-rolled cigarettes called joints, in water pipes sometimes called bongs, or in cigar wraps called blunts. Marijuana can also be brewed as tea or mixed into food such as cookies, brownies, or candies.

> *Marijuana in its natural form is one of the safest therapeutically active substances known to man.*
> Francis Young, Drug Enforcement Administration law judge, 1988

WHAT'S AT STAKE?

What effects might there be on new regulations, law enforcement, or users' habits if a majority of people do not understand the differences between CBD and THC, or hemp plants and marijuana plants? Do you think we have seen this already in the history of cannabis regulation?

◀ When all cannabis use became legal in Canada in October 2018, customers lined up at a store in Saint John, New Brunswick, to buy marijuana legally.

WHAT ARE THE ACTIVE INGREDIENTS?

The leaves and buds of the cannabis plant contain more than 500 chemicals. One of these is called *delta-9-tetrahydrocannabinol*, or THC. This is the compound that gives people a mood-altering feeling they describe as a "high," or "being stoned." Another chemical compound is CBD, which is short for **cannabidiol**. Although CBD can make you feel relaxed and calm, it does not affect brain function and so does not make you high like THC.

The *Cannabis sativa* plant has two main forms: hemp and marijuana. Hemp has more CBD and much lower THC than marijuana. It is the CBD that scientists have found helps people with many different medical conditions such as **epilepsy**, chronic pain, and the **nausea** that comes with cancer treatments. Cannabidiol can be taken as pills, liquids, creams, or inhaled by **vaping**, although this can lead to lung damage.

THE LEGALIZATION DEBATE

Many people believe the growing, selling, or use of any sort of drug should be illegal. They worry about the effects of addiction on families, society, and in the workplace. Others believe cannabis is part of a public health strategy. They say its benefits outweigh any dangers, and abuse of cannabis is less harmful than other substances such as alcohol. Still others see legalizing marijuana as a way to generate a stronger economy by creating jobs, new products to export, more money from taxes, and to control crime related to illegal sales and drug use.

The *Cannabis sativa* plant was grown and used as medicine in the ancient world. In early North America, hemp fiber was used to make paper, clothing, sails, and rope. Its seeds were used as food. Back then, the hemp plant had much lower levels of THC than the plants do today. In the 1800s, doctors used cannabis to treat stomach pain and vomiting.

As early as 1850, marijuana was used to treat seizures and anxiety. But new medicines, such as aspirin and **morphine** for pain, meant the demand for marijuana decreased.

After the Mexican Revolution of 1910 to 1920, many Mexican citizens fled to the United States. Marijuana had been used recreationally in Mexico by people such as soldiers. Their use of alcohol and the drug often led to violent behavior. U.S. citizens against the flood of Mexican **immigrants** linked them to what they believed to be a dangerous, unpredictable drug. U.S. antidrug groups warned of the crimes associated with smoking marijuana and nicknamed it the "Mexican Menace."

AGAINST THE LAW

During the Great Depression of the 1930s, many people in the United States feared and resented the immigrants and blamed them and marijuana for an increase in crime and related violence. This led to 29 U.S. states outlawing marijuana and criminalizing the possession and sale of it.

▼ Marijuana use in the 1960s, such as at the famous Woodstock music festival in New York state, became a symbol of changing attitudes of youth toward fewer rules in society.

◀ The pro-cannabis Society of Mental Awareness (SOMA) organization behind the Legalize Pot Rally in the United Kingdom in 1967 paid for an ad in *The Times* newspaper based on this poster.

The Marihuana Tax Act of 1937 allowed doctors to still **prescribe** marijuana, but everyone involved in producing, selling, and giving it to patients had to pay a yearly tax. This meant many doctors stopped prescribing marijuana. In the 1950s, there were even stricter laws created, with jail time for first-time cannabis possession.

Today, growing hemp—therefore producing CBD—is federally legal in both the United States and Canada. However, in the United States, certain states have created rules limiting how and what type of CBD can be made and used medicinally. As for marijuana—rich in THC—the U.S. federal government treats it as illegal, while several states permit it for recreational and medical uses. In Canada, all types of cannabis use became legal in 2018.

TIMELINE

1500 B.C. Chinese writings show use of medical cannabis
1840 Medical marijuana is widely used in North America
1906 Pure Food and Drug Act requires cannabis products to be labeled
1911 Massachusetts is first U.S. state to outlaw cannabis
1927 Ten more U.S. states pass marijuana prohibition laws
1937 U.S. Marihuana Tax Act
1938 Canada bans the growing of cannabis
1968 New studies show marijuana is less dangerous than alcohol or other drugs
1970 Marijuana is classified under the U.S. Controlled Substances Act as a drug with no accepted medical use
1976 Marijuana decriminalized in the Netherlands
1996 California is the first state to legalize medical marijuana
2003 First Canadian citizen receives government-grown medical marijuana
2017 Mexico legalizes medical marijuana
2018 Canada legalizes growing, possession, and use of cannabis

Much of the debate and laws concerning the use of cannabis separate recreational from medical marijuana. Recreational marijuana is smoked to feel high. Medical marijuana, or medical cannabis, refers to using the plant or **extracts** to treat pain or illnesses. It is prescribed for many reasons. The chemicals in the plant, known as cannabinoids, have been shown to help with different conditions, including:

- Alzheimer's disease
- cancer
- seizures
- eating disorders
- mental health problems such as PTSD (posttraumatic stress disorder).

Many people argue medical marijuana should be legal. However, in the United States it has not been approved as a medicine by the FDA (Food and Drug Administration). The FDA needs the data from studies of thousands of patients to determine if the benefits of its use outweigh the risks. So far, it states that there is insufficient evidence. At least 25 countries around the world, including Canada, have already legalized medical marijuana.

POTENTIAL DRUG ABUSE

Some people against legalizing even medical marijuana are concerned that medical use will lead to more

▶ The effects of smoking marijuana fade in a few hours, but the drug can be found in the body for days or even weeks longer.

recreational use. They are worried about the use of marijuana leading to addiction. Addiction is the intense focus on using a certain substance even if it might be harmful, to the point that it takes over your life. Addiction can lead people to lose their health, their money, their families, even their life.

Some people fear marijuana is a **gateway drug**. These are drugs that may lead to the use of stronger and more dangerous ones. Studies in the United States and New Zealand have shown that, of people who have used cannabis, 44.7 percent never go on to use other drugs. The same study did find, though, that use of marijuana from an early age, and its frequent use, are linked with using other drugs.

WHAT'S AT STAKE?

To what degree should governments restrict citizens from taking or using something that has health risks? If a government can regulate one substance that has benefits as well as risks, should it regulate all similar substances such as cigarettes, alcohol, and vaping?

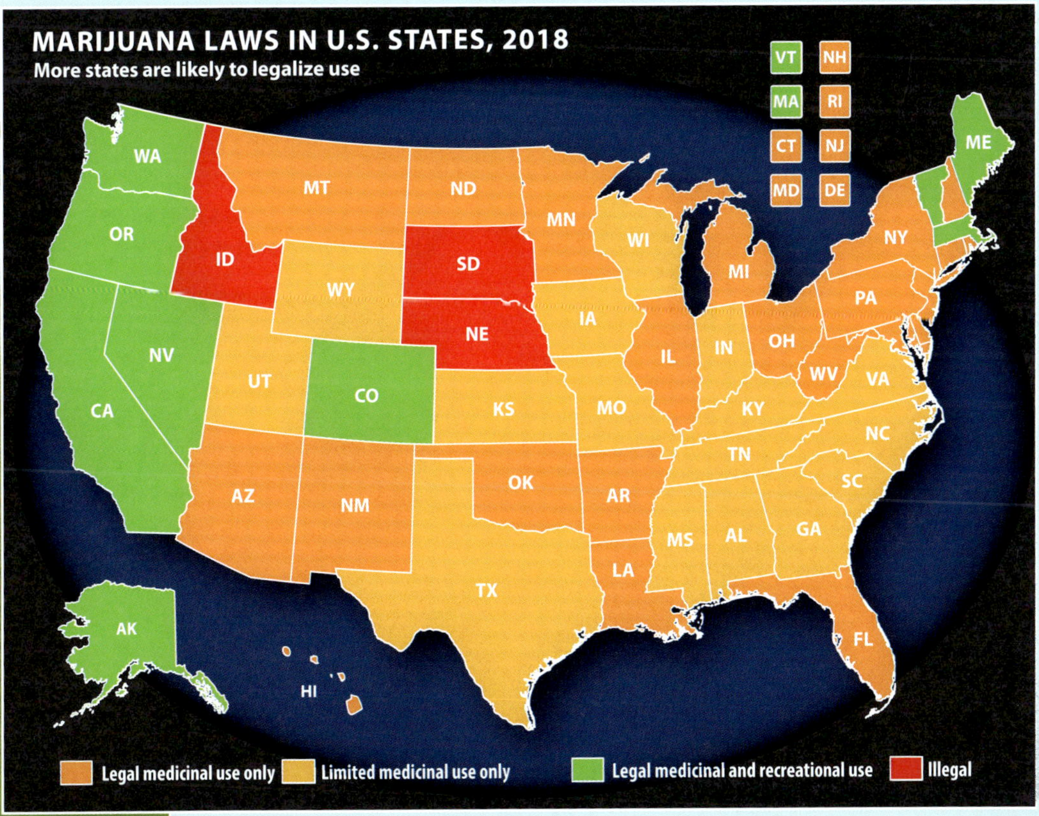

THE WAR ON DRUGS

The "War on Drugs" is a phrase used by governments and law enforcement. Its aim is to reduce the illegal drug trade and eliminate the abuse of drugs, including marijuana, and the effects of addiction on society. It was made popular in a speech by U.S. president Richard Nixon in 1971. The plan was to prevent new addicts and to **rehabilitate** those who were already using drugs. This included those who used marijuana recreationally. It is estimated that the U.S. government spends $51 billion each year on programs for the War on Drugs.

Statistics show that since the War on Drugs began, the number of people using drugs, and the availability of drugs, continue to rise. Most agree that this war has been lost. Some countries are turning to even tougher laws and law enforcement

▼ A woman is arrested for drug possession in Nebraska, where marijuana is illegal.

KEY PLAYERS

Now that Canada has a legal cannabis market, large companies are hoping to make a lot of money by selling it to retailers in huge quantities. The four biggest are **The Green Organic Dutchman Company**, **Canopy Growth Corporation**, **Aurora Cannabis Inc.**, and **Aphria Inc.** These companies are expanding as they expect more demand for legal cannabis products. Huge buildings are being constructed to process marijuana. There is also a big demand for commercial greenhouse space.

A similar development is happening in U.S. states where marijuana is now legal. Big cannabis companies include **Los Sueños Farms** and **Copperstate Farms.**

▲ Bales of marijuana from a drug bust are stacked at a Coast Guard station. Arrests for **trafficking** marijuana have risen in states where it is legal, such as California, as smugglers try to move it to the black market in neighboring states.

to solve the problem. Other countries, such as Portugal, believe legalizing drugs and using the money to educate and rehabilitate is the answer.

Human rights organizations are concerned that marijuana users of **marginalized** and underserved groups in society are arrested and jailed for drug offenses in greater numbers than from other majority groups (see graphic on page 21). They connect the rise in these arrests with the creation of privately owned prisons that make a profit. United States' law also allows people convicted of drug offenses and who are not U.S. citizens to be deported.

A NEW PROBLEM

Canada and some other countries have decided to legalize all marijuana use, both medical and recreational. Statistics Canada has released data that shows in the first half of the year since it was made legal (in 2018), the number of Canadians who used cannabis was virtually unchanged from before legalization. The percentage of people who drive within two hours of consuming cannabis (15 percent) is also unchanged since the new law took effect. What is troubling for law enforcement is that more than half of those drivers (57 percent) consumed alcohol as well. The combination creates a dangerous level of **impaired** drivers.

Governments are deciding to legalize marijuana for many reasons. One reason is to direct the money spent on law enforcement, courts, and prisons to education and rehabilitation. Another reason is to get rid of black-market marijuana and stop the power of drug smugglers and money flowing overseas.

In the United States, some states have legalized medical marijuana and some haven't. Different restrictions on who can grow and/or sell in different states means some legal growers are finding they can get a better price by selling on the black market in neighboring states where cannabis products are illegal. This means instead of getting rid of the black market, it is still going strong.

Cannabis Canada reports that the black market in Canada is down 21 percent since legalization. Legalization has meant that the government can regulate and tax those who grow cannabis. This allows them to fund programs for addiction treatments as well as social programs such as helping the homeless. Legalization means it is also possible to control the strength of

ASK YOUR OWN QUESTIONS

What actions might work to reduce or eliminate the black market for drugs? Does reducing taxes on legal marijuana help or hurt the ability of legal growers to supply customers and compete with the black market?

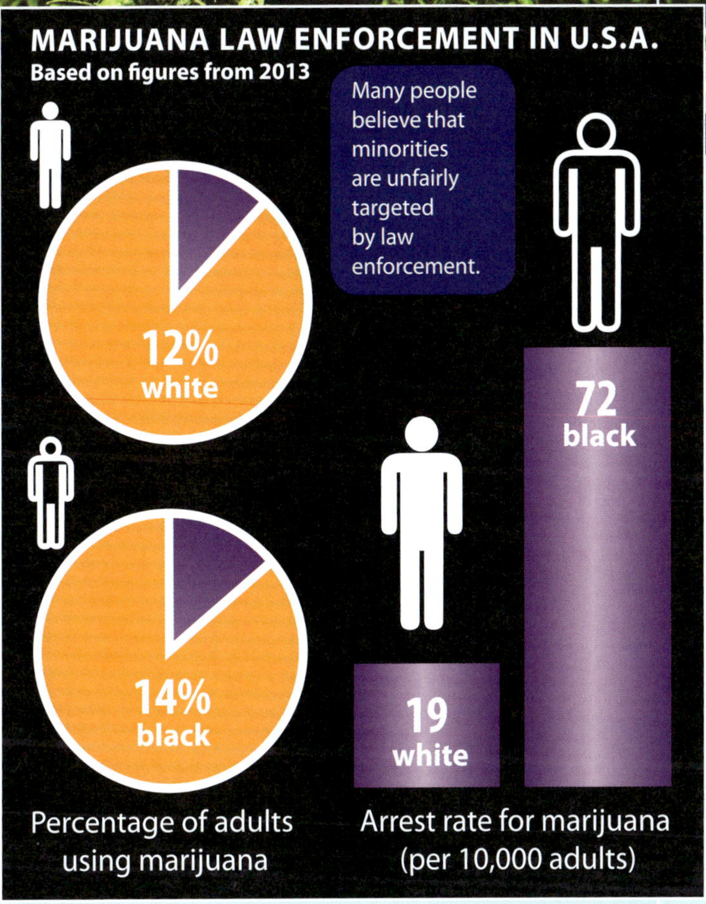

the THC and cannabinoids in the plants. This is important in medical marijuana, where people need to rely on a certain level of chemicals to give them relief.

REMOVING CONVICTIONS

Where cannabis use or possession is no longer a crime, governments need to deal with people already in prison or with criminal records due to marijuana charges. In Canada, there are about 500,000 Canadians with marijuana **convictions** on their criminal record. Bill C-93 was passed by parliament in 2019. The bill will allow people with simple possession charges to be granted a pardon. Simple possession means they had a small amount of marijuana for personal use and were not dealing or selling it. A pardon means the record of their charges will be erased.

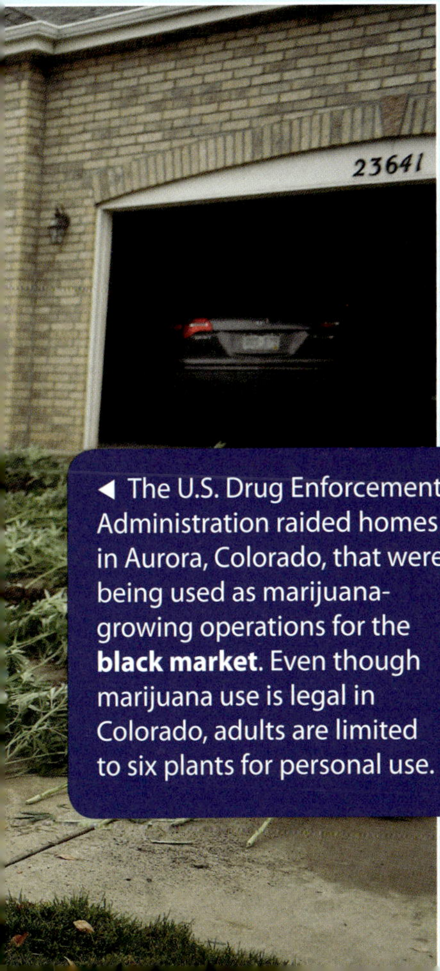

◀ The U.S. Drug Enforcement Administration raided homes in Aurora, Colorado, that were being used as marijuana-growing operations for the **black market**. Even though marijuana use is legal in Colorado, adults are limited to six plants for personal use.

4 SUSPENDING JUDGMENT

Each group in society can see an issue in a different light. To really get informed on a topic it is important to see the issue from all sides. It is best to not jump to a conclusion or form any opinion until you have done thorough research, review, and analysis of all source material.

▼ Action group NORML Canada marches in the Pride Parade in Toronto, 2018. Now that cannabis is legal in Canada, its goal is to educate and protect **consumers**.

One viewpoint in the debate over legalizing marijuana comes from law enforcement. The police and the courts are on the frontline of controlling illegal drugs. When laws change, they are the first to see the good and bad **consequences**.

Police departments hope that with no need to investigate or charge people with marijuana possession or use, they will have more time to devote to other crimes. In Washington State, where both medical and recreational use of marijuana is legal, police report that the number of solved cases of violent crime and property crime has gone up since legalization.

IMPAIRED DRIVING

Police are concerned about an increase in other problems linked to legalized marijuana. Impaired driving means operating a moving vehicle when you are affected by drugs or alcohol. Any type of impaired driving results in more accidents and deaths on the road. While alcohol levels in the blood can be measured by a breathalyzer machine, there is no equipment to test for THC. In Canada, in the few months since legalization, police departments across the country were not reporting any increase in cannabis-impaired driving. The worry is that as the use of marijuana increases, so will the rates of impaired driving.

> *"The marijuana trade is important but it's not the most important drug issue going on in Canada today. Fentanyl kills 11 Canadians a day. Marijuana does not."*
> Vancouver police chief Adam Palmer, October 2018

People suffering with serious diseases, chronic pain, or the effects of cancer treatments see legalization as a step forward in their treatments. They want to see easier access, reliable levels of chemicals, and cheaper prices.

Cannabis and CBD oils are most often prescribed for people with nerve pain, posttraumatic stress disorder (PTSD), or tremors from conditions such as Parkinson's disease. Scientists are also studying how marijuana and THC and CBD extracts might help people with **immune system** problems such as HIV/AIDS and multiple sclerosis. Researchers think inflammation, seizures, and certain mental disorders might also be helped. New studies have found that some of the cannabinoids can protect nerve endings from more damage after serious injury. In Australia, a great majority of 128 people who used medical marijuana for various disorders reported that it provided "great relief" or "good relief."

PAIN MEDICATION

Many people suffering from pain or sickness prefer to take cannabis products over other pain medication, such as **opioids**, because it is safer. The Harvard Medical School says 130

RISE IN TRAFFIC ACCIDENTS AFTER LEGALIZATION

Comparison of traffic accident claims with Idaho, Montana, Utah, and Wyoming where recreational use of marijuana is illegal, for 2012 to 2017.

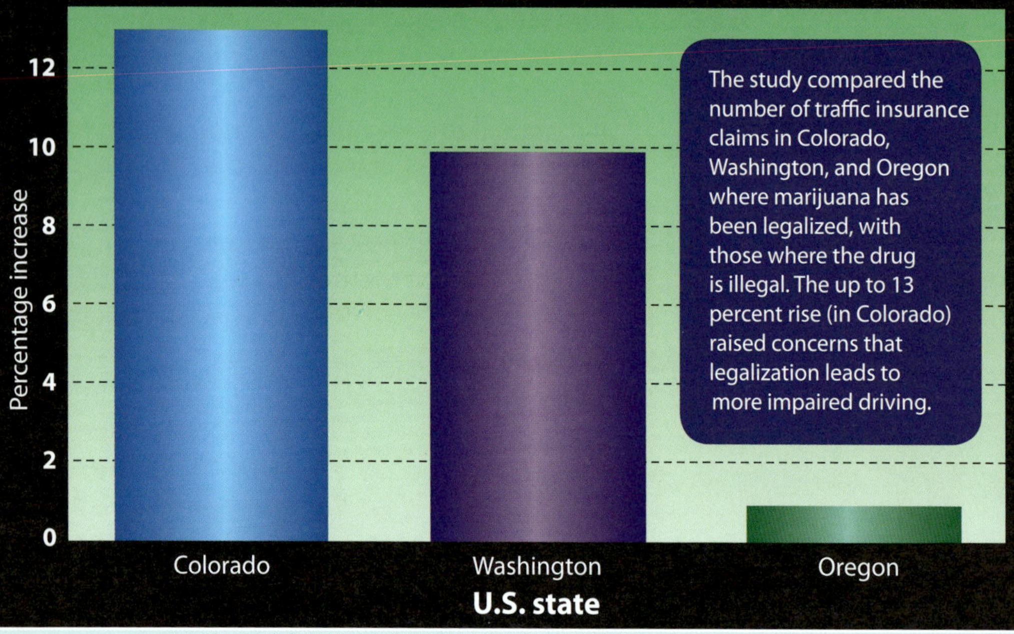

The study compared the number of traffic insurance claims in Colorado, Washington, and Oregon where marijuana has been legalized, with those where the drug is illegal. The up to 13 percent rise (in Colorado) raised concerns that legalization leads to more impaired driving.

PERSONAL STORY

Jody Taylor-Haye of Lake Elmo, Minnesota, was battling severe pain from a spinal disk disease. She was prescribed opioids and other pain medications but after she broke her back in 2014, she became allergic to many pain medications. She tried cannabis-based medicines and her pain level, on a 1–10 scale, decreased from a 10 to a 2 or 3. She now takes half the medicines she used to and no opioids at all.

Americans die each day from opioid overdose, but it is unlikely that you will die from an overdose on marijuana. It says marijuana and CBD oils give patients a safer way to treat pain.

Some people hesitate to ask their doctors to prescribe medical marijuana products because it still carries a negative stigma. Patients say that smoking is often better than taking pills because the relief is immediate. Cannabis in pills can take up to 30 minutes to be felt by the patient. Also, they claim that pills increase the chances of under- or overdosing where smoking does not.

Because marijuana affects several symptoms at the same time, it gets rid of the need for patients to take other drugs that may have side effects. People against legalizing even medical marijuana say some patients are using their health as an excuse to get marijuana.

▼ A study done in 2013 found that CBD can help block the addictive side of other drugs such as morphine. CBD lowers the feeling of pleasure from morphine, so a person craves it less.

COMMUNITIES AND ADDICTION

Communities globally are dealing with a huge drug problem. This has resulted in a rise in drug-related crime, accidents, and deaths. Society sees the debate over marijuana legalization as a part of this crisis. People are worried it will lead to easier access to marijuana, higher rates of social acceptance, and drug addiction, in particular among youth under 18, whose brains are still developing.

Studies show that about 30 percent of marijuana users will develop some level of addiction, and that the age one begins to use marijuana affects the addiction risk level. People who use marijuana before the age of 18 are four to seven times more likely to develop an addiction. Parents worry

ASK YOUR OWN QUESTIONS

When compared to the views on tobacco and vaping, more people in the United States believe marijuana is not at all harmful (see graphic opposite). Where does this perception come from? Where could you look to find accurate information about the dangers of marijuana to make up your own mind?

▶ Many people believe that colorful packaging and appealing images will encourage young people to try edible marijuana without knowing the risks to their health.

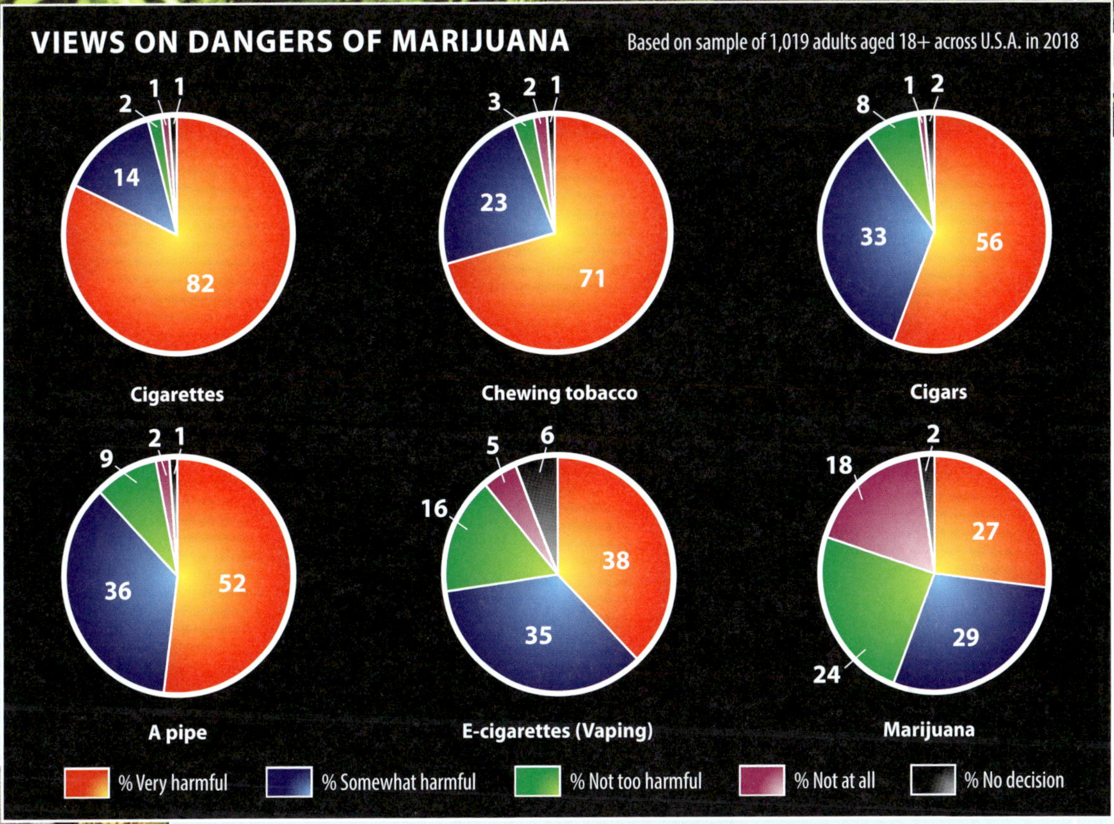

that with easy access to the drug, young people will have greater opportunity to start using at a younger age. Studies by the Yale School of Medicine and the University of Ottawa show that marijuana use by teens can lead to severe mental health issues.

EDIBLE MARIJUANA

Marijuana **edibles** are products baked or cooked with cannabis. Unlike smoking, where the effects are felt right away, the effects from edibles don't peak until a few hours later. This might result in consuming more cannabis than is safe. Products with edible cannabis in them look the same as ordinary ones. Parents worry that it will be easy for it to get into the hands of children who do not know it contains marijuana.

Other people argue that using a less-harmful drug like marijuana will keep users from turning to other types of addictive substances. A study by Amanda Reiman, Ph.D, showed that 40 percent of marijuana users substituted it for alcohol, 26 percent for other illegal drugs, and 66 percent for prescription drugs. They say this will lower the dangers for society from addiction, not raise it.

MARIJUANA EFFECTS

For people who use marijuana or cannabis products, legalization means they can do so without fear of being arrested and jailed. They believe they should not be punished for using cannabis any more than people who drink alcohol or smoke cigarettes.

Those against legalization worry about the message that marijuana use is basically harmless. Studies show using marijuana can result in different effects for a short while after taking or smoking it. Some short-term effects on the brain include confusion, anxiety, panic, or sleepiness. It can also cause impaired ability to remember, concentrate, or pay attention. For some people, marijuana can even result in a more severe

THE CENTRAL ISSUES

Do you think information on the dangers of using cannabis products is easy to find? What would be the best way to educate the public, especially younger people, about the short- and long-term risks of using marijuana?

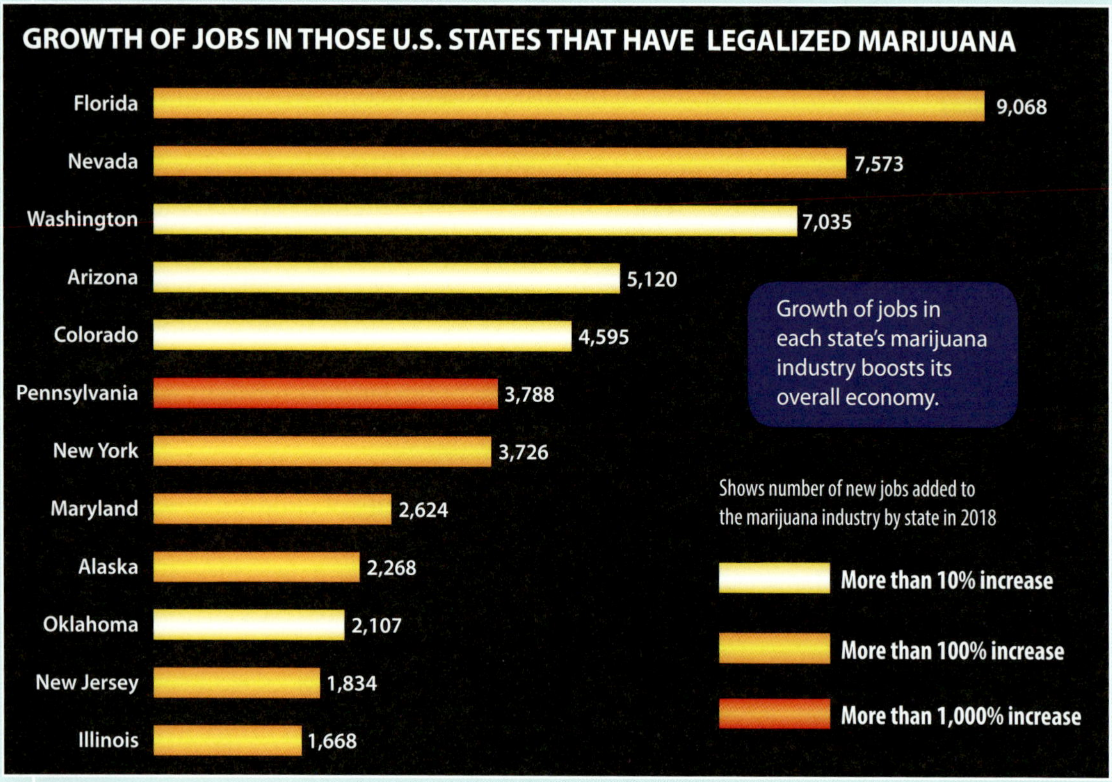

▲ Some clinics are owned by companies that produce cannabis products. Health officials worry that clinic doctors will prescribe marijuana in high doses for all sorts of conditions because the clinic is owned by a company that will profit from the higher sales.

reaction, with **paranoia** and **hallucinations**. The body is also affected by marijuana and cannabis. Blood vessels can be damaged and blood pressure can drop. For some people, their heart rate increases.

LONG-TERM EFFECTS

Research shows that marijuana use has a more serious and long-lasting effect on younger users. The younger the person, and the more often it is used, the greater the risk of long-term damage. It can damage brain function and "rewire" the brain in people under the age of 25. Some of the damage may not be able to be undone. Even for adults, long-term use of cannabis can harm memory, concentration, intelligence, and the ability to make decisions. It can lead to problems with bronchitis, lung infections, and chronic coughing.

Users who are for legalization say legal cannabis is much safer than black-market marijuana. They have no way of knowing what might be in illegal cannabis. It could contain mold, pesticides, or even other chemicals. Legal cannabis will be controlled and tested.

5 WHERE THINGS STAND

The issue of the legalization of marijuana is still being hotly debated. Even where it is illegal, more and more people are using cannabis products each year. This is especially true of **millennials** and people more than 50 years old. As you gather information, you will notice that not all of it is accurate. Misinformation can spread like a virus through social media such as Twitter and Instagram.

THE CENTRAL ISSUES

People holding certain positions or status in society are more easily believed or agreed with than others. Should a **politician** or talk-show host be believed as quickly or routinely as a doctor or scientist about health issues? Should you double-check facts no matter who reports them? Why, or why not?

◀ This photo shows cannabis flower heads and equipment for making hand-rolled marijuana cigarettes or joints.

Misinformation clouds a subject and makes it difficult to make good decisions. The more misinformation is repeated, the further it spreads and the more people believe it. Sometimes people spread misinformation to support their own agendas. Other times they do it without knowing.

Often we believe misinformation because it reinforces what we already think about a topic. At other times, it is scary to accept that what we have believed or heard all our lives might have been based on incorrect information. It is difficult to go against the opinions of close friends, family members, or teachers. Sometimes we accept something as truth because we respect the person saying it or because they are in a position of power. For example, in 1980, then U.S. president, Ronald Reagan, stated:

"[M]arijuana, pot, grass—whatever you want to call it—is probably the most dangerous drug in the United States and we haven't begun to find out all the ill effects . . ."

CHECK THE FACTS

Although there is risk in smoking marijuana, modern science shows that this statement is highly exaggerated. However, many people accepted that as fact without any detailed medical data to back it up, simply because the president said it. It is important to check the facts of any statement, no matter who says it. Remember that an opinion is someone's personal viewpoint. Opinions are not always based on fact. Facts are always backed up with scientific evidence.

CHANGING ATTITUDES

In the last 30 years, people's views on cannabis use have changed. Many people say that attitudes from years ago do not match with current facts and figures about crime, addiction, and health risks. Some people have changed their minds because data showing how the drug could ease symptoms and conditions helped them see medical marijuana as a valuable drug for all kinds of patients. Other people say studies on the effects of THC convinced them that it is not more harmful or addictive than substances that are already legal such as alcohol.

Attitudes are also influenced by learning from countries that have now legalized marijuana. We can see what works and what doesn't. Are laws strong enough to protect the young? Are laws open enough to allow people suffering from diseases or treatments to quickly and cheaply access the drugs that will ease their suffering? Do addiction rates go up after legalization? Do crime rates? Do impaired driving rates? By sharing information, scientists, governments, and health workers can help one another manage marijuana use in the safest way.

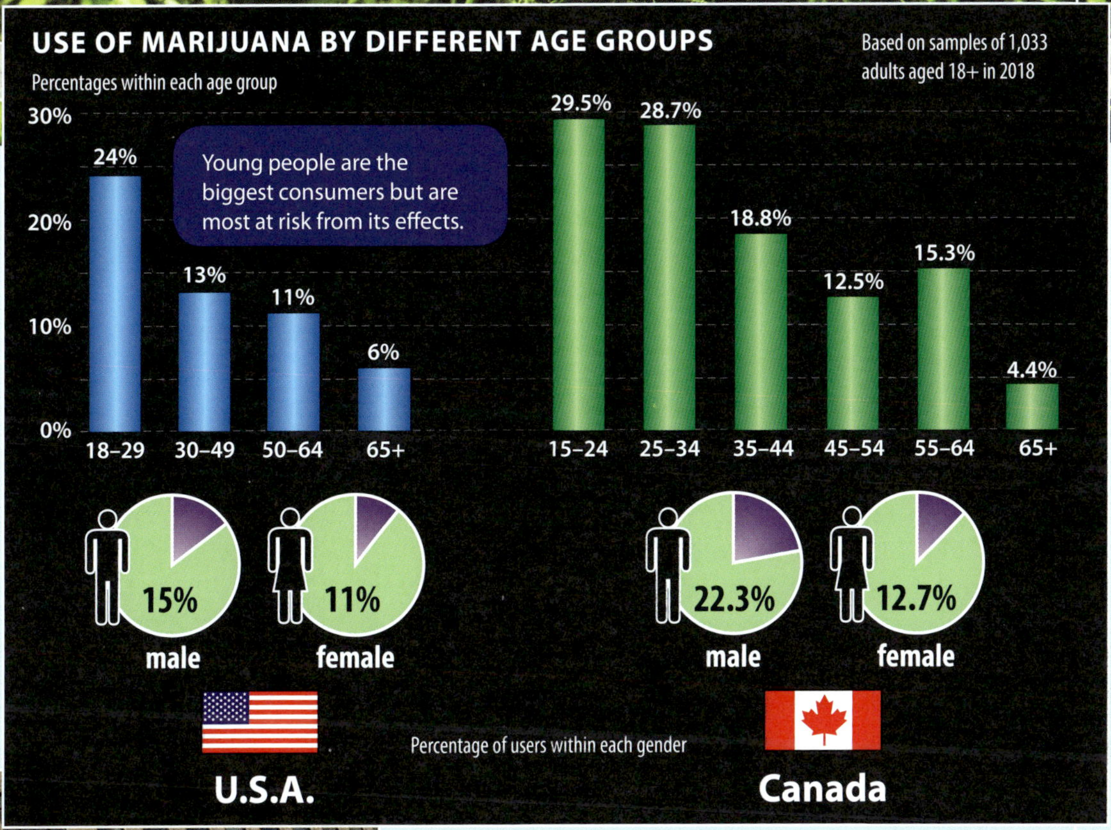

◀ The Cannabis Parade in New York City takes place on the first Saturday in May each year. Its mission is to legalize all forms of cannabis. The event is now joined by sister parades in more than 300 cities worldwide.

BENEFITS AND DANGERS

Current studies show the benefits and dangers of marijuana use. A study at the University of New Mexico showed that marijuana can be very effective in lessening pain. On a scale of 1 to 10, people reported, on average, a drop of three levels after taking marijuana. Other scientists are investigating signs that marijuana use can change **genes** that make addiction more likely. New research is studying whether or not cannabis use changes genes that may be linked to **autism**. These types of scientific studies are vital to regulating who should or should not use cannabis products.

Some people do not change their views even with scientific proof. We have to be able to let go of what we thought was true when new data comes along to prove it false.

It takes time and energy to research a topic or question our beliefs. Some people find it easier to simply hang on to what they thought in the past. Myths are popular ideas that are false. They may be held on to and spread because they sound right or because they have been around for a long time. There are many myths about marijuana that are not backed up with facts:

- **If pot is legal, a lot more people will use it**

The data from countries and states that have already legalized marijuana shows no increase in the percentage of teenagers using it, and only a slight increase in one age group—namely, adults more than the age of 55. In Portugal, rates of youth using marijuana actually dropped in the years after legalization.

▲ In Canada, the government is allowing cities and municipalities to decide not to have retail cannabis stores in their area. Cannabis will still be available online or in neighboring areas.

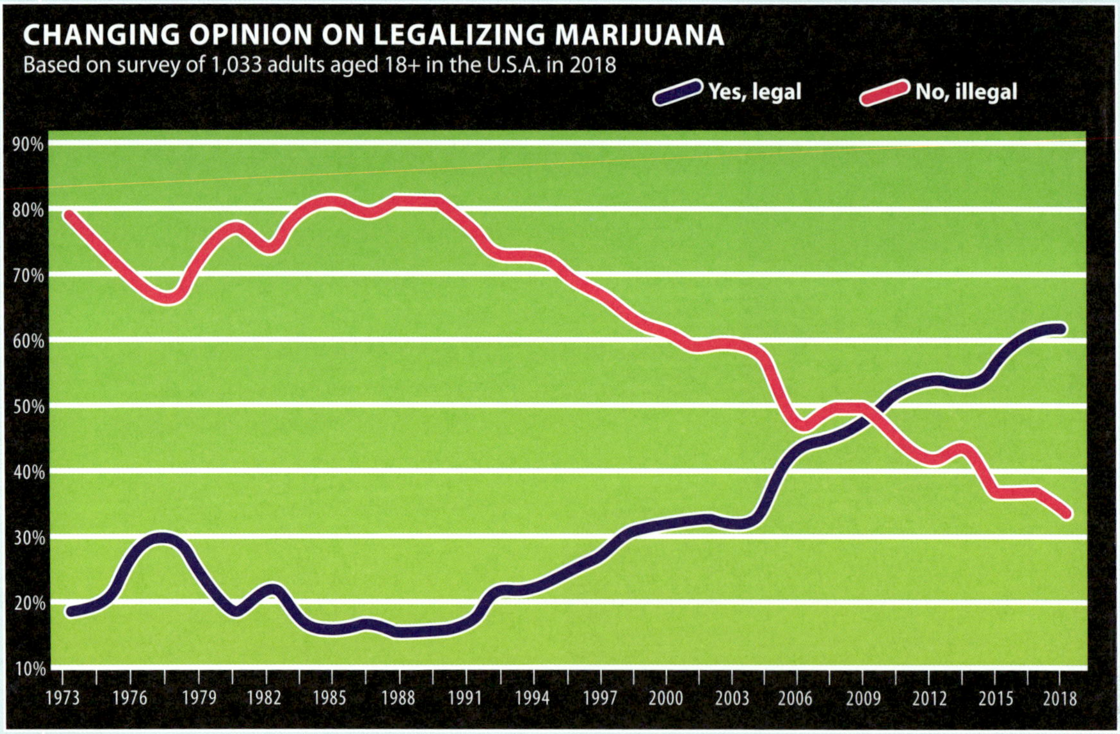

▲ Talking with counselors, health care workers, medical professionals, and parents can help people dealing with addiction issues, depression, and thoughts of possible suicide.

- **You can have a fatal overdose from smoking pot**

You cannot have a direct overdose from smoking marijuana. However, you can die as a result of using it. The link between suicide and marijuana use is strong. There is also a greater chance of **fatal** accidents with vehicles or machinery while high on marijuana.

- **Marijuana is not addictive**

Marijuana is addictive. One in six teenagers (and one in eleven adults) who try the drug will develop an addiction. This is a lower addiction rate than many other drugs, such as cocaine, alcohol, and even **caffeine**, but it is still a problem.

- **Marijuana causes no harm**

Although it is a natural, plant-based substance, it can lead to many problems. There can be breathing problems, complications for pregnant women, and mental illness. Although it is sometimes used to treat anxiety, it can also cause anxiety in some people. It has long-term effects on the brain, especially for people who are young when they begin to use it.

ASK YOUR OWN QUESTIONS

What are some ideas about marijuana use that everyone seems to agree on? Could they be myths? Where can you look to find out more about them?

KEY PLAYERS

SAM, or Smart Approaches to Marijuana, is based in Virginia. One of its goals is to educate the public with scientific facts. Another is to stop legalization and prevent the creation of Big Marijuana (like Big Tobacco) that would market it to children. They also promote research to get FDA-approved, pharmacy-dispensed, cannabis-based medications.

In the United States, there is a **patchwork** of different marijuana laws and regulations that vary from state to state (see page 17). This makes it difficult for people moving around the country and looking for legal sources for their medical or recreational use.

In Canada, researchers are watching closely to see trends in crime and addiction rates concerning legal marijuana use. This information will be used by other communities, states, and countries as they debate legalizing marijuana in their regions. Before marijuana became legal, the federal government stated that one of its goals was to keep cannabis "out of the hands of children and youth."

The minimum age set by the federal

▶ Coffee shops in Amsterdam in the Netherlands that can legally sell cannabis are a popular tourist attraction. No one under the age of 18 is allowed to buy it, and proof of age is required.

government to buy, have, or grow cannabis is 18. Some provinces have set the age at 19. In Quebec it is 21. There are also resrictions on where users can smoke it, for example, no places in or near where children gather, such as schools and playgrounds. Other goals are to make the supply safe and free from chemicals and **toxins**, and to eliminate the black market.

COMPLEX COMPARISONS

The justice system is slow to clear criminal records, and many users are still using illegal street and online cannabis stores because they can get the product quicker. Legal medical cannabis is experiencing delays and shortages as the new system works out supply problems.

While most countries have made medical marijuana legal, recreational use of marijuana is still illegal. Several European countries do not impose jail time when people are charged, just fines. In others, such as Spain and the Netherlands, there are coffee houses or social clubs where cannabis is available to the public. This has caused a problem with large numbers of tourists who visit in order to use marijuana. The number of young Europeans who support banning recreational marijuana is dropping each year, but no laws are being drafted to legalize recreational marijuana now.

▲ Supporters of legal marijuana in Canada made their own Canadian flag with a cannabis leaf instead of a maple leaf.

6 KEEPING UP TO DATE

Finding trusted sources of information on such a hot topic as legalizing marijuana can be difficult. And the consequences of using medical or recreational marijuana can be serious for your health, your family, and criminal record. It is vital that you use good source materials and make the right decisions.

SEARCH TIPS

When looking at websites, address extensions can help pinpoint what sort of information you may be getting:

.gov (government)—restricted for government entities.

.org (organization)—anyone can register for this, although it is often used for nonprofit organizations and charities.

.com (commercial)—originally for businesses, it is the most widely used extension.

Country extensions:
.ca Canada
.au Australia
.uk United Kingdom
.ru Russia
.de Germany

◀ Most young people turn to the Internet for information. Sites where information can be shared quickly allow misinformation to spread.

Much of the new medical information about cannabis comes from scientific studies being done on the various chemicals in cannabis and their effects on our bodies and minds. Some studies conclude that medical marijuana is still not proven to be effective and that more research is needed.

Staying up to date on the latest findings will help you make informed choices. But where can you find results of these studies? *ScienceDaily, Science News,* and *ScienceSeeker* are just three websites that search out and report on the latest scientific discoveries.

Governments and the legal system are always working to create or update laws and regulations that protect the public. Governments at the state or provincial level, as well as at the national level, have websites to follow the latest news. Statistics are also found online at *Statistics Canada,* and at *Data.gov* for the United States.

LOCAL INFORMATION

Cannabis use also has a big impact on society, our communities, and our families. Local news, on television, in print, or online, is the way to keep connected with what is happening in your local area. Information booklets at public health offices, doctors' offices, or in pharmacies can give you current information.

Asking questions of professionals, such as doctors, nurses, pharmacists, police officers, politicians, and teachers, can also give you new perspectives on what is happening or changing concerning the issue.

GET THE FACTS RIGHT

After gathering your sources for information, how can you be sure you are getting the best, most accurate, and unbiased data? Are you getting different perspectives for a balanced view? Are you recognizing bias in what you read or hear? **Auditing** your **news diet** is an important step in staying informed.

Check who owns and runs different websites. Is it a major company, like a large cannabis producer, looking to improve its reputation to keep profits up? Or is it a public health organization such as the National Institute on Drug Abuse? An organization that does not profit from its findings is usually more objective.

ASK YOUR OWN QUESTIONS

How can the mission statement or "About" page of a group, company, or organization help you when auditing your news diet? What different information can you get from articles written about the same groups or companies from an outside source?

CHECKING THE DATA

A pro-cannabis group, such as the Hemp Industries Association, will always have a bias in what it reports to support its beliefs. It may still have good information, but you need to always keep that bias in mind when reading articles. Data from an opposing group, such as Citizens Against Legalizing Marijuana, will show a different bias. Reading or listening to both sides will help you get closer to an objective viewpoint.

Even groups that do their best to be objective sometimes report false information. Double checking facts with a second source is always a good idea. Check if the author of an article or report has any background in the subject. Check with government statistics to see if the numbers are accurate. Red flags are when a person or organization is trying to sell you something, when a report is sponsored by a business or organization that will benefit from one result over another, and data given by someone with no qualifications in the subject.

▶ Typical levels of the mind-altering chemical in marijuana, THC, range from 0.3 to 4 percent. Some strains, however, can have THC levels as high as 25 percent.

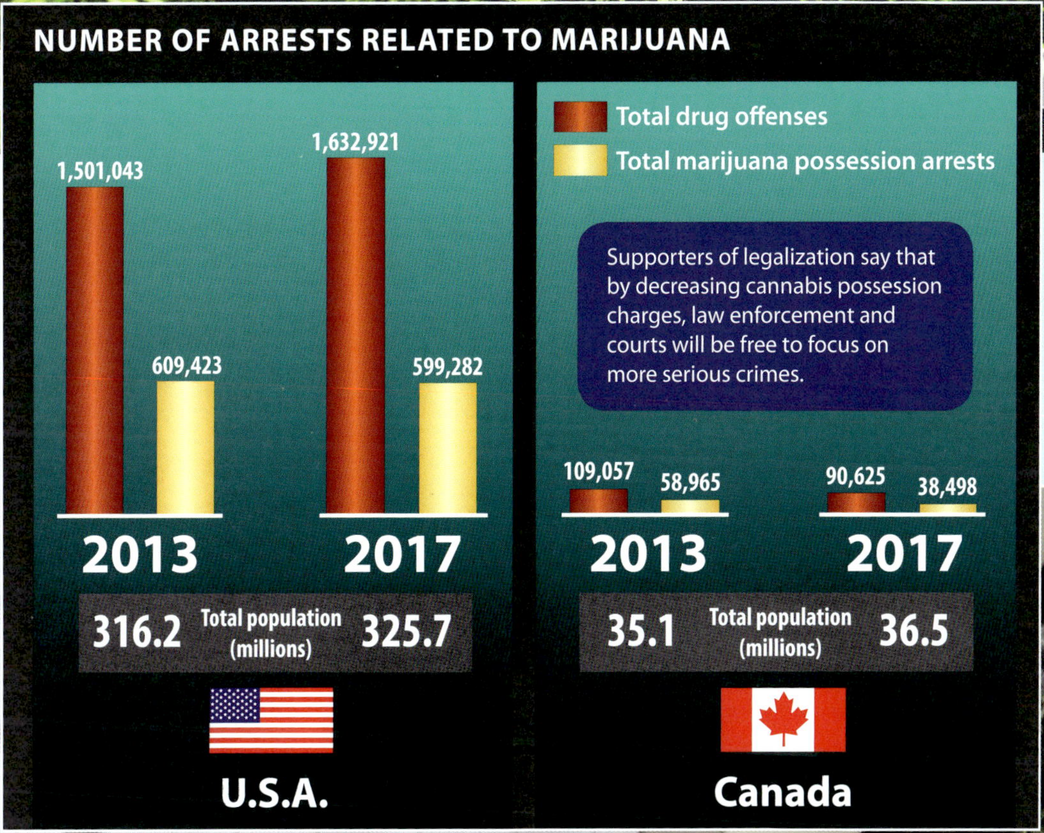
NUMBER OF ARRESTS RELATED TO MARIJUANA
Total drug offenses
Total marijuana possession arrests
1,501,043
609,423
1,632,921
599,282
2013
2017
316.2
Total population (millions)
325.7
U.S.A.
Supporters of legalization say that by decreasing cannabis possession charges, law enforcement and courts will be free to focus on more serious crimes.
109,057
58,965
90,625
38,498
2013
2017
35.1
Total population (millions)
36.5
Canada

WHAT YOU CAN DO

▶ Sharing information with friends or peer groups can help you gain a balanced perspective and lead to new questions to ask.

Once you have become informed about marijuana, it is time to set up a plan to stay informed. It is good to use a variety of print, digital, and audio sources.

Newspapers from your community will show how the issue of legalizing marijuana is affecting the people where you live. Stories might focus on the opening of a new legal cannabis store or on the local police struggling with an increase in people driving while high. Magazines offer articles that go deeper into a subject than newspapers. There are also often interviews with people who are directly affected by the topic, such as families who are worried about their teenagers accessing cannabis from friends or people who use marijuana for medical purposes.

GET ORGANIZED

There are tools online to make it easier to find and get updates from online sources. News aggregators are programs that gather and post news on a regular basis. *Google News, Apple News,* and *Feedly* are just some aggregator apps. Setting up a Google alert is a good way to not miss new reports on a topic. Use keywords, such as "legalizing marijuana," "cannabis," or "medical marijuana," to get alerts when new reports are posted online.

Podcasts are online audio files that you can download and listen to on your computer or mobile device. You can use your search engine to find ones discussing all the issues concerning cannabis. Bookmark any that might be a series so you can check in regularly to see what has changed.

You can also create a file of bookmarks from drug abuse associations or cannabis organizations to make checking them easier. Getting and staying informed about legalizing marijuana will give you the knowledge you need to ask for changes from your government and make safe decisions in your life.

SEARCH TIPS

When searching for a topic, such as marijuana, online:

- Use quotation marks around a phrase to search for that exact combination of words (for example, "medical marijuana").
- Use a colon and an extension to search a specific site (for example, Addiction: gov for all government website mentions of the topic).
- Use the word Define and a colon to search for word definitions (for example, Define: vaping).

GLOSSARY

addiction The need to use a substance even if it is harmful

analyzing Studying closely and working out how evidence fits together

auditing Inspecting and evaluating

autism A disorder that results in difficulties communicating and interacting with others

bias A view in favor or against something or someone

black market Unlawful trade in goods

caffeine A chemical in drinks that stimulates the brain

cannabidiol Chemical compound found in cannabis plants and used to treat medical conditions

citizens People who have rights to live and vote in a country

consequences Results of a person's actions

consumers People who buy products

context Time, place, and circumstances in which information is created

conviction Being found guilty of a crime

decades Periods of 10 years

edible Safe for eating

effective Good for getting the results one wants

epilepsy A condition that causes seizures

evaluate Work out the importance or worth of something

extracts Substances taken from a plant

fatal Causing death

gateway drug A substance that may lead to the use of stronger or more dangerous drugs

genes Part of the information in cells that controls how the body grows and works

hallucinations Experiences that feel real but do not exist

high Feeling good, especially from the effect of drugs

immigrant A resident who has come from another country

immune system The cells and tissues in the body that protect it from infection

impaired Damaged or weakened

intimidating Making you feel threatened

joint Marijuana cigarette

legalization Making something lawful that was previously illegal

marginalized People who are consided unimportant and are left out of events

millennials People born between 1981 and 1996

morphine A powerful pain-relief drug made from opium

nausea Feeling of sickness

news diet The group of sources you use to get your news

objective Based on real facts

opioids Drugs made from the poppy plant, including morphine

paranoia False beliefs that people are going to harm you

patchwork A mixture of different things

politician A citizen's representative in government

prescribe To issue a drug as a medical treatment

Prohibition Time from 1920 to 1933 when alcohol was banned in the United States

recreational For fun and pleasure

rehabilitate To return someone to good health

society Group of people living and working together in an ordered way

source material Original document or other piece of evidence

statistics Collection of information shown in numerical form

stigma Strong feeling of disapproval

Time and Place Rule A rule used by historians to assess how true and accurate a source of information is

toxins Poisonous substances

trafficking Dealing or trading something illegal

vaping Breathing in nicotine and other drugs as vapor rather than smoke

SOURCE NOTES

QUOTATIONS

Page 5: https://www.cbc.ca/news/world/10-provocative-quotes-about-legalization-for-global-pot-day-1.1228862
Page 9: https://www.ctvnews.ca/politics/notable-quotes-about-legalizing-marijuana-1.3958700
Page 12: https://www.calgarycmmc.com/famouscannabisquotes.htm
Page 23: https://www.cbc.ca/news/canada/british-columbia/police-marijuana-legalize-1.4863382
Page 31: https://www.youtube.com/watch?v=VxHBx6H-xFo)
Page 37: https://www.ontario.ca/page/cannabis-laws

REFERENCES USED FOR THIS BOOK

Chapter 1: The Marijuana Issue, pages 4–7
https://bit.ly/2mRaEP6
https://dpo.st/2ooAlXJ
https://www.washingtonpost.com
https://bit.ly/2mUBrKe
https://bit.ly/2oq1Z6L
https://bit.ly/2VcODVV

Chapter 2: How to Get Informed, pages 8–11
https://bit.ly/1mvRHe8
https://bit.ly/2m61fTl
https://bit.ly/2mUGKcC
https://norml.org
https://bit.ly/2nEXzll

Chapter 3: Legalizing Marijuana, pages 12–21
https://bit.ly/2DXh2sF
https://bit.ly/2mR92Vz
https://www.health.com/pain/what-is-cbd
https://bit.ly/1Gr2dND
https://bit.ly/2lprtwy
https://bit.ly/2CDP0nY
https://bit.ly/2jQm0Rw
https://bit.ly/2mSqrgC
https://bit.ly/2hU40Sn
https://bit.ly/2oqyQlJ

Chapter 4: Suspending Judgment, pages 22–29
https://bit.ly/2v2mdDV
https://bit.ly/2ohomem
https://bit.ly/2nDyE8z
https://bit.ly/2mVgUFB
https://bit.ly/1mvRHe8
https://bit.ly/2Ksp52L
https://bit.ly/2nCnwsp
https://bit.ly/2Bqc3Q1

Chapter 5: Where Things Stand, pages 30–37
https://bit.ly/2m6JnYy
https://bit.ly/2mRg6S3
https://bit.ly/2H3Fj0o
https://bit.ly/2mFhRBT
https://bit.ly/2Bqc3Q1
https://bit.ly/2VpOVJc
https://bit.ly/2UgzeVc

Chapter 6: Keeping Up to Date, pages 38–43
https://bit.ly/2HBil4z
https://nyti.ms/2zG8OlX
https://www.thehia.org

FIND OUT MORE

Finding good source material on the Internet can sometimes be a challenge. When analyzing how reliable the information is, consider these points:

- Who is the author of the page? Is it an expert in the field or a person who experienced the event?
- Is the site well known and up to date? A page that has not been updated for several years probably has out-of-date information.
- Can you verify the facts with another site? Always double-check information.
- Have you checked all possible sites? Don't just look on the first page a search engine provides.
- Remember to try government sites and research papers.
- Have you recorded website addresses and names? Keep this data so you can backtrack later and verify the information you want to use.

WEBSITES

Canadian Centre on Substance Use and Addiction:
https://www.ccsa.ca/cannabis-canadian-drug-summary

National Institute on Drug Abuse:
https://www.drugabuse.gov/drugs-abuse/marijuana

The EdCan Network on cannabis risks for students:
https://bit.ly/2nJK9el

Kids Help Phone talks about cannabis:
https://kidshelpphone.ca/get-info/cannabis-important-things-know/

BOOKS

Brown, Brian. *Cannabis: The Illegalization of Weed in America*. First Second, 2019.

Goldstein, Margaret. *Legalizing Marijuana: Promises and Pitfalls.* Twenty-First Century Books, 2016.

Hand, Carol. *Marijuana (Drugs in Real Life)*. Essential Library, 2018.

MacCarald, Clara. *Marijuana (Facts and Fiction about Drugs)*. Rosen Central, 2020.

Ventura, Marne. *The Debate about Legalizing Marijuana*. Focus Readers, 2018.

ABOUT THE AUTHOR

Natalie Hyde has written more than 80 books, both fiction and nonfiction, for young readers. When not writing, she enjoys researching her family tree and feeding her chickens.

INDEX